'cos you're my

Friend

LION
Giftlines

My friend

Not the in-group,

Not the crowd,

Not too quiet,

Not too loud.

Far from stupid,

Not too clever,

My friend now,

My friend for ever.

A true friend knows
the meaning of a secret.

Or else.

When family brings trials,
A friend brings smiles.

Roses are red,
Violets are blue,
Aliens are green,
But not me or you.

I'll be your friend

Till the desert sands freeze

And the camels come sliding home.

And then –

Well, that'll be that, really.

Friend's service station

Homework advice bureau

Gossip chamber

Secret exchange

Floods of tears unit

'Beat the bullies'
briefing

'Coping with families'
counselling

My friend has gone utterly loopy,

My pal has gone quite round the bend.

She's off on a far-distant planet –

Where will her insanity end?

In the words of the immortal bard:

'Once more unto the beach*,
dear friends, once more.'

William Shakespeare

* Some clever show-off is bound to tell you that Shakespeare wrote 'breach', not 'beach', and you say of course, the quote is from his play **Henry V**, and the king was exhorting his troops to go to the breach in the enemy's defences at the Battle of Agincourt. So there, dimwit: this page makes use of a play on words. See next page.

'Once more unto the breach*,

dear friends, once more.'

William Shakespeare

Let us go out together to face our common foes:

fierce beasts – human, animal and teacher!

* See previous page.

A friend in need is a friend indeed.

A friend in need is a bit of a liability.

Mottoes to live by

You can do it!

Give it a go.

If at first you don't succeed, try, try and try again. If you want to, that is.

It's your call.

elieve in yourself.

This above all: to thine own self be true.

Go for it!

And, above all...

you look great!

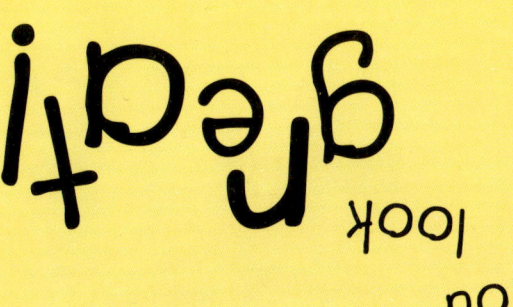